POEMS
AND
PRAYERS
for Our
BRAVE MILITARY WARRIORS

STEPHANIE NAYLOR-LILLARD

ISBN 978-1-0980-1735-4 (paperback)
ISBN 978-1-0980-1737-8 (hardcover)
ISBN 978-1-0980-1736-1 (digital)

Christian Faith Publishing, Inc.
832 Park Avenue
Meadville, PA 16335
www.christianfaithpublishing.com

Printed in the United States of America

To all the active and retired military soldiers, veterans, and their families. Without your dedication and commitment to excellence, our nation would not be the beacon of hope for so many around the world. You all are very special and beloved by so many who admire your fortitude, tenacity, and deep love for our well-being.

To Ed

Thank you for your
strong mentorship, leadership
support, community advocacy
and service to members

Signature
2020

ACKNOWLEDGMENTS

I would like to thank the amazing Christian Faith Publishing team whose knowledge, skills, integrity, and deep commitment to faith-based communities to create space for new gifts and talents that minister unselfishly to others who need hope, inspiration, and love.

I would like to especially thank my family, our military forces, the editors, illustrators, my agent, faith-based leaders, digital outlets, book critics, LegalShield, DHTS, and Unsplashed.com. All of you have provided me with a firm foundation and guidance on making sure I remain focused, humble, and compassionate toward my purpose in God and serving others.

CONTENTS

I Believe

I believe the Lord spoke to me early this morning as I prayed for guidance and understanding.

I believe God is preparing this day to be a blessing for me as I represent the Kingdom in all of my actions.

Thy KINGDOM comes, thy will be DONE as I surrender to his mighty will and protection.

I believe God's will has fervently attached itself to my everyday routine.

I believe the Lord told me to finish this path. The still voice resonates within my spirit as my call to DUTY is upon me this day.

I Need You

*Y*ou really are a hero
I'll tell the whole world, I said so!

It is important that you believe it!
You are in a uniform that represents years of historical, monumental achievements

Every day you rise and fight
I NEED YOU to know that I am patiently waiting for you stateside
Continue to be bold and brave
Many are counting on you to save them from troubled times that have come their way

Put on your helmet, soldier, along with your military-issued boots
I NEED YOU to continue representing our American troops!

Missing You

I don't want you to think that night goes by without you being on my mind
I pray that God continues to be your guide

Knowing the risk you take to make sure we are safe keeps me on bended knees, asking the Lord, please

> Keep a hedge of protection around you…
> Quicken your instincts to connect those clues…
> Sharpen your mind to make the best decision…
> Execute the order with SNIPER precision…

Now wipe the sweat from your brow as it drips down, thank God
You made it to another round

Know that you are special and part of the chosen few
I hope you know I am a proud American who is thinking and MISSING YOU.

Soldier's Song

*T*raining for the unknown
deployed in war zones
A warrior is trained to be ready at all times
Avoiding all catastrophes, constantly looking for troubled signs

Using field intelligence to gain the upper hand
UNITED WE FIGHT, UNITED WE STAND!
We rescue our wounded and salute those who have passed
Continuing to move forward until the innocent are free at last

Marching strong and solid as the sun sets
knowing our military is mighty and ranked the BEST
Even though the nights are short and the days are long, we will continue to fight from dusk 'til dawn
singing the tune of this SOLDIER'S SONG…

NC Winter Wonderland

*T*hinking about you during this holiday season
Thanking God for your bravery and countless other reasons

You dwell so deep in my heart that no mountain, no sea, no continent can keep us apart

You will come home someday soon.
I will sing your praises like a wolf howling at the moon.

This picture represents the Christmas weekend 2010 in my hometown.

I hope to hear your footprints when your plane lands safely on American grounds.

Staying Connected

*J*ust because you are so far away

does not mean our thoughts are not connected every day

As the hours become days, and the days become months

I look at your picture to remember how time stood still

When you declared your love for me and my daydreams became real

That moment keeps me warm even though the forecast is a cold thunderstorm.

As the storm passes through the sky, I smile at the memories and take a deep sigh.

What about the time we held hands

I remembered them gently embracing mine

Starring into your eyes with a smile so kind

Every time I see the American flag raised high, its symbol truly respected

It gives me the courage to STAY CONNECTED

As I Was Leaving

*A*s I was leaving, our paths were about to cross

you were fifty feet away walking toward me in the distance

I imagined we made eye contact and passing glances in a manner that was persistent

I wondered secretly to myself if the outline of your lips and the hue of your skin was as beautiful as your heart that beats from within

Your physical characteristics complemented the military uniform that I saw you in

Your stride was effortless and distinctive

The look in your eyes was sharp and engaging

I immediately felt safe just because of your presence and unforgettable essence

When I finally got to my car

I sat for a moment and prayed if I ever saw you again

God would present you as my shining star

As I am reflecting on that wonderful vision

One must cherish every moment no matter what title you hold which distinguishes your position

When you are in the presence of our American military

Even though their job may seem scary, just know they are special human beings

I wish I would have said thank you as I was leaving...

I Love You, My Love

*T*he thought of you brings a warm smile to my face

I anticipate my days being filled with memories of how I long to be with you in a loving way.

I think about what it means to hold our hand, hear your voice, feel your heart beat against my chest as I remember your warm embrace.

I know you feel me thinking about you because my heart flutters every time I whisper your name out loud into the quiet stillness

Each place I revisit to capture the essence of those organic moments I hold close to my mind and heart in this space. God, grant me inner peace from above. I LOVE YOU, MY LOVE.

Take My Breath Away

I am completely in love with you.

Looking so amazing in your uniform on this day,

Serving our country with honor and integrity.

In combat, even when the air is filled with missile smoke and the skies are gray, you TAKE MY BREATH AWAY.

Because of you, I continue to live in a country defined as the land of the free and home of the brave

I wake up every morning with my civil liberties in a land so sweet, my country 'tis of thee…I thank the heavens above

With these lips of clay…baby, you TAKE MY BREATH AWAY…

I keep staring at all the stars in the sky thinking about the love of my life, praying to God, please keep my soldier Alive.

I asked the divine to dispatch your guardian angels to protect you at all times…sweetie, just know I admire all that you do to protect us each day…beloved, you TAKE MY BREATH AWAY.

Beautiful Mind

I see a powerful military warrior who *will not* pass me by.
They can hear my thoughts sing like a lullaby.
It creates happy energy and synergy between
two cognitive demands at first glance.
Quick like sound waves racing across the universe, touching
all the skies. Reassembling images passing by my third eye.
Blue notes are all I see dancing around me in a heavenly form.
Excitement is RIGHT NOW like the rays of a new sun at dawn…
My heart is racing to catch up with my thoughts
as they lap around me at lightning speed.
The sound of their voice gave me no choice but to whisper quietly
how pleased I am to see their thoughts staring back at me.

Faith Alone

*P*itfalls are designed to test those destine to be greater than their circumstances dictate at the time.

The Universe has called you out because there is a purpose MILITARY WARRIORS have been chosen to fulfill and thus becomes your greatest destiny.

A destiny of what is not revealed at the time, but multiple recurrent tests provides a glimpse of itself at every level if you are paying attention.

There are a twist and turns along with *walls of emotions* at every level.

These *walls of emotions* are virtual forts that can encapsulate the body and hold the person of destiny's mind in suspended animation for years until it penetrates the heart and seeks instant death at times or slow, horrible prisms of dark light to slow down your run toward the light of promise, thus forcing the person of destiny to scale the dark pathway using FAITH alone.

- ▣ Faith alone becomes your substance.
- ▣ Faith alone become your light.
- ▣ Faith alone becomes your source of life.
- ▣ Faith alone become your hope.

My Brave Military Warriors

*T*hrough the thunder, rain, snow, or sand, here comes our mighty soldiers flying in the sky and marching strong across the land
-Fingers on the trigger
-Fingers on the computer
-Fingers on radio buttons in the bridge
-Finger on the stick in the cockpit

As they echo READY to brothers and sisters in their unit
-Heart beating fast
-Heart beating strong
-Charging at the enemy with guns drawn
-No backing down until our enemies are gone…

MY BRAVE MILITARY WARRIORS are humanitarians rescuing refugees. Rebuilding war-torn countries before they leave… Teaching them to be strong and arming them with tools to independently address their own insurgent storms. MY BRAVE MILITARY WARRIORS, continue marching on…

The Dojo II Effect

I did not know what to do after being dazed and confused. He was a Marine that taught me how to pursue my dreams without fear and without walls as he stood six feet three, melanin with a smooth bald head, pretty teeth that enhanced his dashing smile.

His presence was undeniable when walking into a room, quickly being acknowledged by all the high-ranking military leaders who were all well groomed. Each flanked with phenomenally strong and beautiful spouses as they danced or nodded their heads to the melodic musical tunes.

It was my first time being invited to the annual Marine Corps Ball. In my delight, as the night progressed, I imagined every hour was filled with steps of success, prestige, and honor. My heart began to be mesmerized by the euphoria of the atmosphere. Oh dear, he was coming toward me as my heart raced with excited fear…

My eyes widened with anticipation as he spoke to me with a commanding voice of stimulation. He quickly grabbed my hand as other members of his team escorted their dates abruptly out of the venue in our ball gowns. An announcement from the BRAVO commander, stern and strong, said the night would not be long as duty called, and our loved ones were leaving at dawn.

I salute and respect their commitment to their nation, along with their band of brothers and sisters in their unit. Seeing them whisk away in military transportation and back to their stations left a sinking feeling in my chest—where do they have to travel to next? I replay the beautiful time we shared together and call that memory record the DOJO II EFFECT.

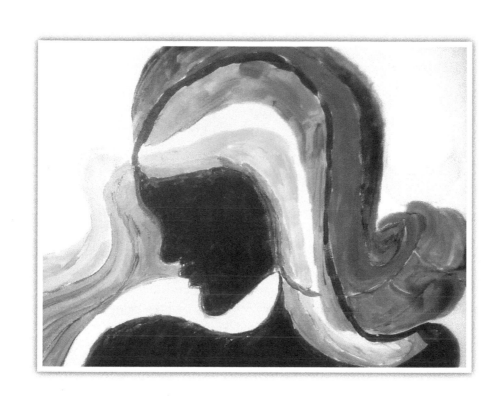

ABOUT THE AUTHOR

$\mathcal{S}$ tephanie Naylor-Lillard is the author of the poem titled "40 Minutes by Flight" and has written her first of twelve volume series *Prayers and Poems for our Brave Military Warriors*, which will focus on active duty and retired military veterans and their families. Her deep love of the military was developed as a child being raised by her father, who served in the United States Airforce, and over half of her family members have committed themselves to the United States Armed Forces. She is uniquely qualified to share experiences as a former wife of a decorated Navy Seaman, former caregiver to a Marine Corps sergeant, and mother to three children who respect and honor our military. She is the president and founder of Global Innovative Solutions Inc. and serves as a volunteer hospital chaplain at Duke Regional Hospital. After pursuing her master's in business, project management, and information technology, she is in the process of completing a dual master's and doctoral program to become a licensed clinical social worker where she will focus on providing services to military members and their families.